CRYSTAL SE

Crystal Set Dreams

MIKE HARDING

PETERLOO POETS

First published in 1997
by Peterloo Poets
2 Kelly Gardens, Calstock, Cornwall PL18 9SA, U.K.

A catalogue record for this book is available
from the British Library

ISBN 1-871471-66-4

Printed in Great Britain by
Latimer Trend & Company Ltd, Plymouth

Contents

After the Wedding

Honeymoon gone she'll stand on silent nights
Watching her breath bloom in the cold yard-light
As falling stars scratch the lampblack sky
And by the stove, lapped in sacks, dry
And warm a coddled sick lamb breathes
Soft milky bubbles on the rug, and she sees
The years ahead stretch farther
And more curious than the questioning stars.

A Month of Angry Skies

New lambs lig on hail, yarl for dams
That sniff the wind sensing ice. Clouds
Spill and rear up pawing at the light.
The sun hangs low, a pewter blister on the world's rim.
Storm coming, the sheep paw the earth, nervous, tired,
Long winter curdling into sour spring.
Dead lambs and yowes melt into the sodden earth,
By walls rot where they fall.

Against the black clouds picked out by the sexton sun
On the dark hill, sheep are foam flecks on moss,
Maggots on Helm Knott's giant corpse. Only
The crows are gorged and rattle in their sticks,
Cackle, sated chevrons roosting. Beyond, the Howgills lurk,
Merging thumb-rubbed into the carrion sky.
And new lambs lig on hail.

The Art of the English Murder

And they were trawling the city's Sargasso,
In the midnight's shining, fast as fishermen,
No oilskins, just a drab tweed jacket and a fake fur coat.

"Like a drink son? D'you smoke? Go ahead.
It's cold the night right enough, d'ye want a lift?
Yer sleepin' rough? We've got a warm wee bed."

Black ice on the tongue, St.Elmo's eyes,
Waiting, seeing no sea nor any star-lit thing,
And then, from somewhere deep and still, surfaced a smile.

How many nights, a sprat in their city's pond
Had I swum out beyond or through their nets?
Liston's, The Rembrandt, Nick the Greek's, the Union,

My sea lanes echoed theirs, shifted by tideswell and pot luck
Chance currents sided me into slack water,
So that bright lobby and incongruous axe,

That sudden world's-end shift from new found mate
To the Hammer House of Horrors sailed on by.
And, slick ships that slid by softly in the night,

The fishers of men moved on, shooting slick nets upon
The shimmering, lamp-washed streets, their siren song —
"Name's Ian, this is Myra. Want a lift home son?"

The Burning at the Crossroads —
a Hebridean Dance

The bat-black wee wild man with white
Wings hung like a long dead gull about
His throat conjured up a kirk-storm. Foam
Frosting his lips he ripped the air
With the jagged jig of his song
And divined demons in the sea-dark room.

And shuffling in the pews, boxed men
Wriggled to the reel he spewed and then
The women slowly sashayed to the lashing hornpipe of
His righteous wrath, as he called down
The Dancing Lord as witness and
Some sour, dour tune rang in the kirk that day.

Stone fiddlers, sabbath dancers frozen in
A ring crowning the heaven-bent hill
He advocated as rock-proof solid of God's
Hot hatred of the catgut and the squeal
Of rosin, the clouded strings, lust in the fingering
The thrusting bow ramming damnation home.

Then men renouncing music took
Their fiddles at his bidding and
Bonfired them at the crossroads, the
Vampire-stilling, suicide-welcoming
Crossroads. Scrolls and soundposts,
Horsehair and ebony, boxwood and abalone;

German fiddles brought by sea-home husbands,
Orkney fiddles won by galley boys and
Home-island fiddles made by slow, quiet men
With salty bulbs for fingers, tinder all: their last
Mad music now the crackling jig
Of driftwood on their pyre, last dance

The eightsome reeling sea-wards sparks
A blush on the air, that shudders to
The fire's strathspey. And fiddles by
The hundreds burning, singing of
Silent weddings and a church-black Harvest Home.
A future when from other islands

Carried on a free sea breeze
Light as spindrift there will come across the sound
Strains, lilting airs lovelier than angels,
Skimming the tips of the waves,
Fashioned only by a fisherman's fingers
A pine tree's blood and a horse's tail.

The Butterfly Men

After ten hours work trudged miles,
Threading the edge of light, ranging gill and syke,
Flitting along crags made brass-gold, gun-
Metal men burnished by the tumbling sun.

Loom chrysalids, their minds unfurled by the mill bell's ring,
They burst out, haloed in the weaving-shed door.
In a mist of light and lint they climbed onto the moor
To catch and cup breath's wing.

Layrocks on the wind's summit riddled out their song
As the golden men walked freedom's edge along
Nets swooping like unreal birds,
And the killing jar did its work.

Later, pinned and fixed and cased
The autodidacts viewed the kill,
Their brittle trophies, flying jewels now still,
Brief fluttering glory stopped and fixed in glass.

And cruelest, mocking Liberty, the rub,
A montage of moths from all over Lancashire,
A showcase central in the room above the pub,
A picture 'All done in our own free time,
Four hundred hours of work, twelve hundred pins,
Four ounces of shellac, gum arabic' and all
To show 'The People's Hero from Italy's far shore,
Garibaldi and his Redshirts crossing the Alps —
Made from more than three thousand lepidopterae'.

City Churches

One's a props store, one's a warehouse,
One's a health club/keep-fit gym.
Windows barred now keep the thieves out,
Keep the sweets and fat men in.

Pumping iron in the transept,
Fourteen daleks in the nave,
On the altar "Chewy Whoppers",
And Transits park upon the graves.

Civic names are carved in marble —
Councillor Higgins in the showers,
Alderman Webster masked by Rollos,
And in the sauna the Reverend Flowers.

Now they give assisted massage
Where they once gave Sunday School,
The only "missionary"'s a position,
The Baptistry's a Jacuzzi pool.

In the place of veneration
"Chocky Bars" and titillation,
And walls that once echoed to Moody and Sankey
Resound to squeals of hanky panky.

Crystal Set Dreams

I walked the sour, sooty, after-school fogs of dank Novembers
When street lamps burnished the yellow world. By amber
Slicked cobbles I crossed the city, seeking out the golden well
Of shop lights near the pigeon market, where the smell

Of hot wax, solder, flux, warm bakelite and triodes,
Glowing rubies in their dusty cases, rolled
Together in a secret sacred litany of joy. Ohms,
Anodes, micro farads, a code as cryptic as Ogham.

Superhets and crystal sets, coils and di-pole switches —
Hilversum, Rejkavik, Athlone, Lyon, Droitwich,
A rubric real as Latin, my schoolboy soul rehearsed —
And for a bob the whispered business of the universe.

A glass pyx of geranium, a cat's whisker frozen
In the alembic of the third form alchemist,
Transmuting swirling gibberish, unholy ghosts
Into bright tongues in the bedroom dark. The Goon Show,

Luxembourg, the Ovalteenies under covers with the bedsprings
Aerial trawling the carrier waves for the gossiping
Of space. And the sounds would ebb and flow
And always in the dark the dreams would come and go,

Dreams on the air waves, dancing, pulsing, surging,
Elusive, fading: hinting at the hand to come that searches
Still, scanning the ether now for other answers; inching on the dial,
Fine tuning the pulsing copper coil, the faintly echoing glass phial.

Curtains

The way he drew the curtains irked you so,
His magazines left on the seats of chairs,
His bubbling pipe, the broken mouse-turd trail
Of dried hard mud from his boots up the stairs,

His cough before he spoke and those old lines
"Well worse things happen at sea", "Fair doos!"
And "Cheer up, you're a long time dead!".
But now as you Oxfam his clothes and shoes,

Those Christmas ties he never wore,
And bin his "comics" and his tarry pipes,
What would you give to find those shards of mud,
The morning curtains hanging "just not right",

A chip of cough from somewhere in the house
Before "Love have you seen my . . . ?"

The Devil's Bible

She called it as outside in the mid day street
The Beelzebub-black, bubbling tarmac
Crackled in the high summer's heat
And sin sizzled in the knave of spades
I used to vanquish the queen of hearts.

Spitting in the grate her peasant faith
She rattled the rosary and clutched fist-tight
To Banshees and the little people,
The bleeding host, the Halloween faces in the firelight,
Hare lips growing in startled wombs and

Holy wells where rags and crutches sprouted.
But Lucifer lurked in the pack, touted
On corners where the ramblimg street boys gambled.
Old Nick, he knocked in the mill-pond pump-house
When valves clacked and we ran screaming

Through the gibbering dark. Holy water fixed him,
Crucifix he cowered before. He slumbered in a city sided on
A lake of fire. More terrible, he was the man who came
At the death of light, hoofs hidden in his boots,
His tail tucked up and horns safe under the brim

Of his everyday bowler. I crossed my arms over
My chest to sleep and street lamps flickered on the sick-
Fever swamps of the wall. All night hell howled in the toy box
And the Rupert books. No solace. Old Nick,
The Prince of Lies and Darkness, Lord of the Flies,

Old Satan who on stormy nights sought out his sinner friends
Ringing the bells of Hell at me beneath the sheets
As he flapped and knocked and rattled and howled
And rasped his privet-twigged fingers all about the house
Trying all the doors and windows for my seven-year shaking soul.

Drunkard

Though I am poor, with you I hold
The star-spattered sky in my hands as they cup
The water of the cut beside the pub.
Though I was cold, bitten, gnawed by the night wind,
I now am warm and burning
With your brazen glow in my belly.
I have swallowed the sunset, engulfed a golden sea.
I, poor, dull fool, am possessed of wit, silvery
Words spill mackerel-shoaled from my lips.
My dull, plain face is dusted with the beauty
Of a lonely house reflected in a rippled pool.

I clutch the glass in my hand and taste
Today, knowing that tomorrow
Yesterday will lie on my tongue like moss
On a wall, weed on a weir:
And in my cold bare room a face will
Look in from the mirror of another room,
Wondering at the mystery of it all.

Fireweed

Where the worst of the city
Laid its rot not caring if
Its brick skirts trailed in the muck
Of croft bomb-site and railway-yard canal and tenements

And a river of purple poison where rank
Rats slid from the bank
And splashed into a crust of yellow foam
A yard high,

Somehow in the cinders, Rose Bay
Willowherb flung up its rags
And made beautiful in a way
This world of scrap and slag.

And when at summer's end
The shaking streets baked in
Hot stones and slates and flags,
Then Fireweed flung its feathers above the town.

That day the clouds, the seeds of Fireweed,
Took to the air, and fumes,
White flames, the smoke of summer,
Swirled in the dancing thistledown streets.

The Fishers

A length of bamboo knocked-off one dark night
From Old Man Corkett's prize allotment plot
In the whispering, fumbling, fear-furred dark;
A bobsworth of line, a float and some split shot,
Hooks and dyed gentles and then we were off.
Away to lodges where mythologies of pike
Lurked in the weeds, or cuts where obese roach
Were always just that one more and one more
Last cast away, forbidden pools where steel-
Blue monster perch had straightened out men's hooks.

We sat for hours willing the float to bob
With all the dreams of scruffy school-less summer days,
Sensing deceit and rumours on the quill's windy twitches.
In winter with chapped thighs saw sun rise like
A belisha on a dye works pool where cat-ice and
A mist a good yard high hung round the chimney bottom,
And lingered drawn and filmy round the rusting presses,
The weed-skinned rotting rollers in the yard.

We sat on towpaths in a summer heat, while fat dull bees
Half drunk with pollen clambered in the soft bell mouths
Of dusty flowers as we drowsed almost to their croon;
While beery men with proper rods smoked pipes
To keep the midges off and lobbed great clouts
Of ground bait out across the rustling reeds
With spendthift workday shovel-hard hands
On a day off from the choking, tunnelled streets.

All summer we came home past sunset,
Tired and hungry, doped and dazzled with the smell
And stench and ooze of it all, the solid heat,
The honeycomb mud, the lead-still ponds
That held the mammoth, golden lurking gods
That lay below the mirrored water's film,

Sensing even then the certain knowledge of
Life and death held in balance on the thin tip
Of the rod, murder in the sudden knock of the quill.

The Flowers of Salford

They had the pick of the bunch that year,
Nineteen fourteen, the lads who marched
Behind the band as streets and factories
Came out to cheer and wave,
Were fit and rough and hard; tough dock donkeys,
Moulders, turners, shunters from the yards,
Pit yackers, brickies, flaggers, navvies. But they turned
Poor Arthur down. When he stood all nerves
And grey white goose-skin in that high
Cold room, the Jock M.O. who held his balls
Flinched from his graveyard breath.

"Rejected", he said glumly to his mates,
"Bad teeth. I didn't know they wanted me
To bite the chuffin' Krauts." But soon the flowers
Had all been harvested, the Somme's
Grey reaping had garnered them all in.
And it was time to pick the ragwort and the dock,
The Old Man's Beard, the clock o' clay, and Fireweed,
White lilies were the Salford flowers then.

Soon anything that had a pulse was gathered up:
Boys and tramps, the short-sighted and the bent,
The hump-backed and the hoop-legged,
Anything to make a bunch, and Arthur went
Stepping proudly, breathing fouly to the front.
Within a month he lay in ragged lumps
In the Flanders slime, compost
For coming poppies, not having
Gnawed one single German.

The Green Man in the City

Long after the mixers and the stalking birds
Of the giant cranes had melted into rust
And the names of mayors and aldermen and kings
Had been rubbed by rain and wind into faint
And shadowy echoes on the naming stones
Naming none but dust.
                              Long after the sons of sons
Of grandsons of the navvies who had laboured here
Were gone, and the men who held the bonds
And stocks and equities were fading ink swirls
And their stories lost; the little fingers that
Had started picking on the first day
Broke through and the green coils licked
Their way towards the light splitting
The streets, tendrils tearing
Silently the reinforced town,

And concrete continents began
Slowly to sunder, drifting. Rift valleys opened
With cliffs of offices as streets dissolved
Under the ivy's lick. The mountains of the banks
Brought down by the battering heads
Of the Fireweed, the wrecking balls of thistledown,
The dynamite of dandelions.
                              And birds
Strangers to this city slowly feel
Their way amongst the streets, nest in
The empty doors and eat the fruit
That hangs from hawthorns in the boardroom.

Hands of the Country

As she sat in her chair staring in the fire
I traced my four years finger along the roads
Of her hands, the valleys between the knuckles,
The hills of bone that rose

Over the slack satin-skinned plains.
I travelled with my child's touch
Along the byways of those old veined
Hands, following, without knowing it

Lanes that would lead down all the days
To the hand that holds the pen
Mapped now with the tracks and ways
Of my own far country.

Haytime

Do you study how many times you'll do this again?
How many hay-times by the river's edge,
Mowing and turning and baling and loading,
Leading and stacking, mowing and turning,
Footcocks and jockeys, sledgeloads and barn,
Back wracked, hands leathered by baling twine?
Sun's teeth gnaws the nub of your neck,
Salt smarts your eyes, crusts your back,
Sheens your belly, cleggs ravage you as you swill
Your face in the cool beck where dippers
On toe-tips, stalk, shot corks from the bouldered bed.

How many more hay-times? Do you think
That as swifts garner gnats, dark boomerangs
Orbiting the barn. A curlew wails fell edge
A rimlight sun shadows an owl on the thorn,
Moon over Helm Knott and the last load got.
Home trundling, your boy running in front,
Your father slow behind brings on the dogs,
As the pulsing of the tractor slices through
The dusk. Across the dale men work by lights
Fields still to get, their engines muted to
A soft moth's burr.
                        How many more before
The boy before is you — you, he behind
Thornbent, with stick and leggings coming on
With the old dogs, following hump shouldered
Crooked by the stone magnet of the land.

Hermit, Shingo La

Halting below the pass,
Sixteen thousand feet, the snow line
Our eyeline and the ponies
Hobbling through. We looked back
To India and the Barai Na La. A sky
Carved from copper salts bowled across
The valley, rocks echoed thought
And nothing moved but the wind dancing
Across the col to Zanskar dusting the sky
With a rag of ravens.
And then a yellow clout in the corner of my eye,
Bending and rocking on a cliff-face ledge
A thousand feet below.
A monk at prayer before a cave mouth,
Snow leopard, bear and wolf for company,
In all this space and air, a dust speck of monk
Spinning out his song,
Weaving it with the song of the stones
And the song of the snow and the raven-punishing wind.

Holland's Bulbs

One of England's glorious dead
Grinning, the eyeless corm that was his head
Found by a springtime spade
Turning the Dutch clay where he had lain

Nearly forty years since that other spring day
When the lurching plane,
Fabric and spars had sucked its way into the sky
And rendezvoused as the searching night

Beckoned them out towards Essen.
A bomber's moon had grown full and brazen,
Bloated and sick with blood, hung
In the black pot of the night. They had sung,

Joked, each conscious of the seeds of death
Filling the plane's pod, their breath
Steaming in the cold. Over Minden, flak
Scribbled itself on the black

Chalkboard of the night. History lesson begun.
Boys with death at their thumbs
Edge the breath's hair of pressure that says
This street dies not that, that stays.

Then flak, fire, the screams of roasting boys.
Oh they were glorious then! A firework feast, a toy
Comet roaring through the shimmering sky
That stretched out over salt-marsh, poldar, sluice and dyke.

*   *   *

Now the fine white bowl of a skull
Looks up at the blue Dutch sky, one slowly turning gull.
And a man wipes his face and sees the rotten
Cloth in fragments round bones forgotten

By all but three or four. An old man, an old lady
And a woman no longer young, who lifts
A picture while she dusts in Hull.
In Holland the man covers the soil over, fits

Tulip bulbs in the moist tilth and prays
Silently under a slowly gyring gull.

In the Dressing Room

He waits, rubbing a finger through thin hair,
Picking a flake of scalp with a broken nail
And sees, within the dark pool of the glass
The face that has taken him all his life to make
Look back across cup rings and fag-end burns.
The years and cities, other times and pains
Are plastered thick with paint, and crease and line
Go deep below the smiling mask until
Only the eyes are left. These motley cannot hide.
They scream of sweated nights in one bulb rooms
Lying in bed beside her, listening to
The clatter of night engines shunting on the croft —
A stranger's body bought with smiles and lies.
They speak of darkness and the cold,
Slick drama played on streets where lamplight dies,
Apron of bare stone flags, the world of props.
Those eyes look back from void into a void.

The cue-call comes, he pushes back his hair
And lurches on the stage, another one
Fearful of that still pool in that dark room.
Clutching his script in the curled fist of his mind
He melts in scenery and lights, becomes the thing
And loses for a while the cancer of his self.

Khumbu Glacier — Nightfall

Across the ice, a white tower bloodied
By the alpenglow. The ice creaks unhurried,
Ploughing its way towards Lobuche.
Hooded seracs sentinel groan.

Tents are wedges on the snow,
Cocoons of freezing breath,
And over the horns of the still world
A slick, brittle moon slides.

Sleep comes hard if at all, stars crackle
Over Sagarmatha and the wind
Blows snow, sly flurries drifting
Against the tent wall.

Any prayer you know would be lost
In the singing of the ice, the hum
Of the Earth's hub turning.
Half-dreams rattle their bells,
Munching at the night, giant
Snow yaks are devouring the world.

Kissing the Moon's Reflection

Bending over the boat's skirt,
Tipsy, to lip the face in the lake, he slipped
Into the pool and sank dwindling,
Melting in the moon's full-mouthed watery kisses.

And lovers on the ink-dark tarn, beneath the cliff,
Moon-faced and moon-struck,
Heard the splash of her embrace.
The echoing ripples licked their skiffs

And lapping, softly rocked them.
"A big fish far away jumping for love,"
Said a young scribe, his fingers
Teasing the nipples of the paper-merchant's daughter;

As the moon as though stemming laughter
Reassembled her trembling, poet-kissing face,
And a fussy breeze rattled the blossom-clotted boughs
And sent pale lips of petals skimming across the water,

Kissing the Moon's Reflection.

Li Po, Chinese poet, (c.700-762) "a lighthearted winebibber" drowned while drunk
kissing the reflection of the moon in a mountain lake.

Lear in Dentdale

Turning sodden grass, rotten, greying
Man bends, back twisted,
Echoing the kink of the fell, hands on the rake.
Sullen as stone, the day breathes
Clammy cave's mouth mist.
From the south clouds roll. The rake's
Wooden teeth bite mush
And the footcocks stand, rot
In the snot-rag size meadow.

Wringing a living from the sour land
His eyes stare unseeing at the stile
And me half over. The hay time
A tragedy greater than Lear's and
The fear of backend with no hay
Got, none to be had,
And worse, a winter that could come
Early, stay late and leave with spring melt
Drumlins of corpses by the Galloway Gate.

Leather

The smell of it was a flower head
Erupting in the room. I loaded jotter,
New pen, rubber, pencils, ink bottle,
Ruler in its maw and it breathed

Out cherry red, new, nutty leather breath,
Echoes of boots and belts and heels and soles.
And I thought of the hunchbacked cobbler in his cold
Dark shop stitching with wax and thread

Its now bulging skin. That first September day
The dwindling summer sun gave way
To Arctic corridors and the Lady Chapel,
New boys, acolytes with caps and shining satchels.

And we sang our *Tantum Ergo, Salutaris Hostia*
And we memorised the complex code,
The new tribe's mythology, the fences of its law.
Caps outside school, no running in the Lady Corridor.

Fence childhood's mind? I ran and a white collar
And red cumerbund soon taught me that leather
Had another use, another smell; the tawse battered
My shining palms as Our Lady looked down from her corner

Her tears painted, mine real. And the marble echoed
To the smack of hide on skin as incense drifted
From the chapel door, the priest glared, the black strap lifted,
And I learned that 'leather' is a verb also.

Swallows

The swallows are putting the deckchairs away,
Laying a tarpaulin over the land with a murmur,
Quavering-fussy dotted crotchets on the wires.
Passing, I sight read 'The Last Rose of Summer.'

Then they are in the air, 'chucking' in counterpoint,
Trying out their wings over Rottenbutts Wood
Where leaves are trimmed with a pale tint
Of rust, a hint of this season's newest fashion.

The swallows muster all along the dale.
In the evening cool they clot, swarm and cluster,
Sensing the summer beginning to fail.
They scissor the softening light

Scenting limitless plains and cobalt skies,
Hearing, on a Dales' wind, whispers of Africa.

Li Po at Black Foss

Climbing down below the crag's
Keen chiselled edge,
He halted by the force where,
Pooled in a water-cut basin of stone,
Peach blossoms waltzed,
Dazzled and dappled in flakes of ledged light,
Before sluicing over the bowl's lip
To slide off into the unknown;
Joining lost loves, lost friends
And the smells of many a summer.

Lost Empires

Saturday mornings as a rule,
Regular as Sunday school,
The dark, red-plush maw of that glass mountain
Swallowed us in one great gulp,
And the celluloid pied-piper took
The children of the red-brick
Web that was our world,
And bound us in cocoons of flickering light.

Hopalong hopped, the Stooges upstooged
Each other, Jeckle heckled, Alfalfa laughed,
Popeye bopped Bluto, Tweety was
Nice as pie and Sylvester the cat
Each week outfoxed a fat Churchillian dog.
There, in those caverns of earthly delights,
We trod the lanes of fantasy, we rode
The range and shot the stars,
And our tiny legs spun faster till we flew
Above the world and all its Emperor Mings.

Now the Bijou, Globe, the Luxor and the Star
Are bingo palaces, new, desperate, fantasy domes.
Old ladies with thick stockings
Holding veins like knots of worms,
Men whose eyes are duller than clay alleys
Queue and shuffle through the door.
The Empire is a supermarket where
I watch a rag-nerved mother with a trolley slap
A little child. Strangely there is no funny
'Tom and Jerry'/'Our Gang' noise,
Just the real and daylight sound of a small child
Whose world, for all that morning, in one stroke,
Has turned from Popeye and the Stooges to King Lear.

Mapping Auschwitz

To   supplying steel hinges . . .
To   supplying stationery notepads,
       typewriter ribbons (various) . . .
Item   indelible pencils (various) . . .
Item   thirty tattooing guns . . .
Ink   for same . . .
To   material cloth, yellow . . .
To   fitting rubber door seals . . .
To   lengthening rail platform . . .
To   300 finest leather dog collars . . .
To   similar quality leashes for same . . .
Sir we tender the estimate below trusting . . .
Sir it is with respect that we submit . . .
To   firebrick for chimney lining . . .
Sir it is with respect . . .

Merman

The seaweed did it — got caught up
Knackered, struggling like a seal pup
When of a sudden the perfidious sea
Spewed me into the net.
What a morning whoop and a holler there was!
Prod and pinch and kick and carry,
Stone cell-flags and them all peering
Calling in their gibberish through the bars
And a man in black, a cross in one hand,
Chucked holy water with the other.

They put me in a creek for fear I would die
Before the freak-show master came,
Iron staves and net to fence me in
And children moon-eyed, dirty-faced
Stared, squeaking, shrill and nudging through the fence.
Two men on watch with a bottle and their pipes,
The moon rose over the headland and one swipe
Of my tail beneath the sleeping boozers' nose
And I was out to sea under a hunter's moon,
Leaving behind only a trail of phosphorescence,
A carving on a tympanum and a stack of winter's tales.

Mills in the Fog

Along the autumn valley that chillblown, chillbrown day,
Fog meshed and wove about the mills, until
It took the bottom windows in its grasp
And spun out spars and twists of amber light.

Then, mills cast off and loomed above the mist,
Like tall ships tugging at their moorings. One
By one the gaslamps bloomed and hissed to life,
Became puffballs of fiery orange steam and soon

Only the tallest windows cast their lights,
Fine trembling warps into the weft of fog.
And mills sailed off down rivers of dank mist
As hidden lorries snarled and lumbered past.

Worlds trembled in the leaf-hung drops of fog
And the wet breath of the darkness took the day.

Nodes

For what else did they scale the hills, grub out caves,
String votive rags round wells where solid
Music chanted on the cauldron's lips?
For what else did they corbell hives from the Skelligs' flesh,
Knouts paternostering their backs, encoding their dreams,
Cuchulain meshed with Christ?
For what else did they lie facing the west, looking to
The dead king lying in the sea? For what else did each day
The hot sun cast the caul of clouds
To slip into the waves, the moon rise pared to a rind
Over the lapping lips of the world?

A sinew, nerve, tugs under all this stone,
Runs beyond the coils of thought, the scat
Alleys, the libraries, the catacombs
Of crusted, clotted words that sink
Under their own weight,
Falling half way to the mark.
Under it go the nodes, peak-seekers divine.
Bare foot they scrabble up the rocks
Breath flowering in the cold Atlantic air,
Segged hands span the wand,
Hazel twitches, feels the node and knocks.

Odds and Sods

We trembled it seems on the touchline of our lives,
Huddled in the penalty box.
Every games afternoon found us shivering in line,
The also-rans, the overlooked, the too fat,
The too thin, the asthmatic, myopic, anarchic,
The cack-handed, the swots, the dopes, all
Hoping to be picked for the house, not a hope,
Not a lousy chance.
                          Odds and sods
Sixteen a side on the worst pitch, with a patched ball.
'Get on with it!' the priest said to us all
As he ran to referee a proper game. All afternoon one lad
Leaned up against the goalpost reading Joyce,
Let every sad goal dribble in, another scribbled poetry
On bits of paper. A fat asthmatic boy
Scored an own goal, fell over and moaned about a stitch,
Then lay flat down examining the clover.
                                        Odds and sods.
While across the playing fields the pukkha teams
Played up, played on, for Catholic England,
House against house in the name of the saints.

Calls came across the autumn frosty air 'Come on Chads! —
Up Albans! — Lose that ball now lad!
Play up St Wilfs! — Oh! Well played St Cuths!'
We ran round kicking soggy spiritless leaves and mud
Knowing that the game wasn't worth a bloody
Chapel candle. The fat, the thin, myopic, gay,
Athsmatic, poetic, day-dreamers — still out there
Punting the balls of destiny at shifting
Imaginary goals, with ghostly, priestly voices
Shouting 'Right you bods
Pick out two teams now — odds and sods.'

Oliver's Hammers

1.
Wheezing, Old Willum back-handed
Young Limping Thomas. It landed
And he smarted so much that on his first
Job a year later vengeance burst

Open the block, Tom's rag-capped
Head nodding as the chisel rapped
And riddled, grizzled into the grain
And another Old Willum was born again.

Toothless and nattering, leering out,
His shining head would wear as cap a grout
Of mortar and a flying rib of the Chapter
House. Other angels and gumboiled tappers

Stopped to watch the guying. Next,
For a virgin in the transept,
A girl who lay with Lambkin,
Her innocent face kiltered on the edge of a wink.

Cack-handed apprentices too fast for Thomas's limp
He chiselled them as yammering imps
To plague the damned who hung and fell,
Stone bait, dropping down the fish maw of Hell.

A glazier with a boozer's orange-skin nose
Became a Jack in the Green, rose
Out his rock-leaf bower to glower
Half-pissed into the chapter house

And children came to marvel and squeal
And women came from backstone and wheel
To stand, a huddle of gawpers,
In all the chippings, lime-dust and mortar.

2.
But time chipped more, the minster grew,
And he became Old Limping Tom, and cheeky new
Raw 'prentice masons modelled him in gutterspouts to wear
Pigeon droppings in his limestone hair

As he sat in the lodge wheezing
His songs into the fire, singing of the past,
Bones locking and the whispering dust that glazed
His lungs gripping his future fast.

3.
Then, one hard blue October day, thick-wristed lumps
Of farmers turned by Cromwell into critics stumped
Into the church and rapped their ringing hammers
On the singing stone, playing out new, stammering,

Model canticles in the echoing choir. Noses,
Oak leaves, angels, green men, roses,
Fell in showers of stone, and wings and glass rained down
Snakes and dragons and the women (bags of dung!),

Whatever frenzy could fetch. First Kristalnacht,
The sky fell to the floor, the heavens cracked
And tintinabulations of cobalt and sea-green, ruby, indigo
Dropped. That day the roof snowed jewels, and motes of rainbow

Dust floated through shafts of new, brash, heretic light
Long after the shattering and the laughter stopped.
That day the outside world looked in on dunes
Of lead and tracery in the desert of the ruins.

Where clouds on Calvary once were frozen bright
New clouds raced on a reeling sky, Christ
The pelican had flown and jackdaws spanned the space,
Apse, ogee and squint their nesting places.

All luscious lights from branch and root
Gone, and the reredos, wood whorls all booted
Into crumbs, a pogrom against joy
And colour turned the world November grey.

4.
And in it all Old Willum lost his nose and he looks now
On coach tours, students, children from the town,
On video cameras and bomber jackets with that same sly grin
And the scars of Oliver's Hammers on his chin.

On Such a Night

The moon slips over the fell
Through a tear in the sky
Of bruised and hurrying clouds and balloons upwards.

On such a night men watched
The legion clanking toward Tor Dyke
A winter solstice in the offing.

On such a night, Noll Cromwell lugged
His cannons under Barkin Fell,
A flashflood took one wagon and a horse away.

On such a night Fox jagged towards Briggflatts
His lathered horse blowing frost clouds into the dark,
Drinking at the silver-skinned beck.

On such a night the souls of the dead
They believed burn waxy in the sky.
On such a night men died and maggots danced.

On such a night under such stars,
Abraham and his didi koi
Camped outside the walls, sparks
From their fires furling to heaven and
Flowering for a second,
Red stars mingling
With the ice-blue specks in the desert sky.

Railway navvies by their fires
Pissed on hands to harden them
As owls under this same sailing gong of a moon
Hunted grandads of grandads of voles,
That would tremble
At night bombers coming back from Germany
On such a night.

Owl and the Photographer

I flew away to the rotten elm
To watch. A hotch potch of gear lay
On the forest floor. Then
He went stumbling noisily away,

Leaving a little house. Now when I fly
By night there are murmurings
And the dark canopy
Of the wood is bright with quiet lightnings.

Owl and the Shrew

Held on the wire breath of the air
I follow planes of my own devising.
Not so much silent as a black hole in
The noise of the night-whispering wood.

Slicing the air I fall a sudden hammer.
The last thing that you feel
A shift in the air and the sense of
Darkness thickening.

Shadows and Footprints

And when you had gone
On those long summer nights
I still could feel
The shadow of your touch,

The press of your arm on
My chest light,
Spooned to me heeled
And cupped.

And now alone
Your echo in the white
Sheet still printed, kneels
Hutched, a core,

An ammonite of love on
The pillow pressed, night's
Breath left, as real
As dinosaurs.

Sheffield with Roses

A warren of mean streets, the station left,
Roared past us, clicked like frames of film.
One row, long, red dull brick and dim
Ran with the train along the tracks
As we pulled slowly out. The yards
Bin-full, with pale dim huddles of wet rags,
Bald mops and worn sandstones. House after house
Rolled by till one, just one house in the row
Alone was a burst, a carnival
Of colour and roses, roses, everywhere
Were spattered all about that yard.

From old paint tins and buckets rose trees grew
And filled the yard, crawled out across
The broken pigeon loft and rambled round
The door where one old man stood on his step,
Shaded his eyes against our windowed sun
And watched the train and people passing by
His life. And he alone stood in a fire,
A hosanna, a benediction
Of wind-twitched roses, summer-burning
In a waste of brick and slate and soot and slag.

The Song of the Flute

Blow a breath into me man, lip to ebony lip,
Make the quick air thicken, pulse and hum;
Tip and roll the tune, your fingers flickering up
My spine and let reel round the room

My throbbing soul of wood. Blow root to branch, core
To twig, and heart to arm to wrist to fingers' cran.
All song and breath; echoing the winds roar,
As he shouts in the branches, howling off the land,

Battering the soft heads of the waves.
And the set dancers on the harbour flags weave
And wind to the tune's tickle and shout. Man, chance
A flutter of wood-song, tap-root dance.

Such a small stick in the hollow of your fist,
Come lip to lip, and let us, lovers, kiss.

Stone Saints

Coming to the bones of the Island
They scraped and scoured them clean,
Winning a grudging tillage from the rock.
To bury their dead they made stone chambers,
Playing card cairns that could crush
An army. Here slept kings whose wanderings
Were the matter of songs.

Monks fired by dreams born in a desert
Turned songs of Oisin into Christ
And, unlocking the vertebrae of this sleeping giant,
Piled rocks in beds and beehives, crawling between sheets

Of Atlantic air to clutch at sleep
That was a dream and dreams that were
Half air. Aislingi ceol on the winds,
The sea swallowing the sun in the
Wet maw of the west.

Later they took tools, tapped
Away the skin and found beneath the faces
Of saints. Facets of the light showed
Snapping demons, Sheila na Gigs and
Spewing beasts caught in the spangled watery light of the west.

Family Album

1. SUNNY MEMORIES

First the Box Brownie gathering sundust memories
Snares a small boy with a paintbrush
Playing with water pretending to paint a house door.
And what the camera sees down all the years
Is a hot summer's afternoon. Even through
The half tones of the snapshot you can feel
The warmth peel off the brick and rise towards you.

Then baggy shorts, swaddies grinning by a tank,
Tin hats-cockeyed two fingers to the blank
And endless African sky. While behind them
Alexander's desert reaches beyond Memphis
Into a future of factory whistles screeching
Through grey winter's dawns.

Next Blackpool, the tower, fag in mouth, his head
Cut off above the eyes, the soldier grins, his arm round
A girl who squints into the sun. Behind, a baking day
Rolls forever up the beach and one ancient donkey plods
Along his old accustomed reach with the same
Small boy upon his back.

Then a garden plot, snot-rag sized,
A blurred baby toddles towards a ball just before it falls
Fixed in silver salts. The song freezes the bar's measure
Frozen at that pitch, feeding back
Into the unsung future.

2. LEAVING THE NORTH WALL

In the half tones of the dawn
Cattle caoining and wall-eyed
Their hoofs crackling on the cobbles
As they were loaded, stumbling,
You stood with bundles, half a handful
Of you, herded. 'Country people' the gardai said
Grinning as the gangway sipped you up
And away in the grey dead light.

Once out beyond the point and the buoys,
The Sugar Loaf diminishing,
The coast a rumour of grey green,
The great whale of the ship bucked towards
Liverpool leaving behind in a
Trail of hissing foam the whispered
Images of the past.

The railway station and the waking crowd,
The shy handshake at the Sorrow Bridge,
The chip of stone from the hearth, the bottle
Of water from the well, the cob
Of turf from off the reek, and fields of
Stubble, hay time done with neighbours
Straightening up and waving as they gathered in
The gleanings. All of this hissing
In the wake that feathers out into the mist,
Bubbling silver becoming swelling lead.
The boat's butting snout
Rutting blindly towards the foreign years ahead.

3. THE TAILOR'S THIMBLE

Mr Levenstein the Jew you are surprised
To find a decent man. His people killed
Your Christ and yet he smiles, is good to girls
Who are ill or whose children are not well.
The cloth slips through in a river
And day on day the river flows.
Bolts and selvedge all new words to learn
Treadle and treadle and sing and oh!
The bright new money on each Friday night.

And outside the oily pane, the Salford light
Smoke grey, the great skies of the West
Seem a dream, treadle on and treadle on.
Eyes that levelled out along a turf bog edge,
Looked to where the hill met Atlantic clouds,
Now guide the cotton under the yammering spike
And the cloth slips through in a river
And day on day the river flows.

Diaspora's children — Levenstein, O'Neil,
Goldman, Pyne, Quinlan, Tobias.
And one morning passing for some cloth
You notice the Hoffman presser's great right hand
As though someone had stitched on
Another from a bigger man.
And the cutter later that week
Loses a finger and the cloth acquires a sunset
While the machines lilt on
And the cloth slips through in a river
And day on day the river flows
Into a world that to you is still but names
Chalked up on the dispatch door:
Sudan, Karachi, Tanganyka,
Madras, Capetown, Lahore.

Talking to the Wall

Passing the window this Spring day,
I stopped and looked out at the wall, seeing
The late sun sculpt out every course
And joint and capstone, through and post.

New lambs called out beyond the lane,
Late walkers hurried to the pub,
The jumbled syllables of bootsteps counterpoint
To homeward-going cracks of flapping rooks.

So wall, we finished you. You'll 'stand
A hundred years', said John, rubbing
The snots of mortar off with a thumb
As tough as tup's horn. So, a hundred years

On and some other eyes will look out through
Another afternoon like this,
Sensing the murmuring day turn, sun-
Sodden towards the edge of light.

Smoke no doubt will filigree as now
From houses down the dale.
And the watcher at the window, standing
As I stand now, will perhaps wonder at the wall

A while, wonder who built it, perhaps wonder more
At men building their walls to outlive them,
Will think of numberless hands and miles
Of wall, will shake his head and turn

To lay the table, just as I do now,
Listening for his family coming home.

The Unfortunate Tongue

Tell tale tit, your tongue will split
And all the little birds will have a little bit.
— Children's rhyme

Not just the famine-blackened tongues
Alone froze, the emerald floss of gnawed
Grass rimed on their thin splintered lips;
For other townlands, hearing the bog whisper, hiss
The hex of Irish, took to mumming. So the hunger dumbed
The living and the dead. To say the words
Was to conjure down the curse, new Babel blighted
While fat corn-full ships wallowed in the sea roads
And *an feár gata* trembled in the wind. Numbed,
What could they do but take and kiss
The colonising tongue and leave the old
Words to the mumbling women at the pump
And the mountainy men who still drove glass-
Eyed stumbling cattle through Baal fires
Made of bog oak? To leave it all to the bog-
Locked islands of the Gaeltacht and the wooden
Shameboard *an bata scoir* about a child's
Neck? To leave it all to the coffin ships
Leaping the rolling waves taking with them
Lost lexicons?
                                    But under all, the new
Thesaurus and the future's gloss, still a fierce beauty
Slumbers like a bog fire, echoes on the wind,
Outcalls the untrodden grass and swinging cottage doors,
And paraclete flames lick here and there:
A murmur, a song flickers, a chant, a spark
Jigs, catches tinder until there is a fire to spread,
Out-calling the caoining of the gulls.

Note: *an feár gata* — the Hungry Grass. A kind of fairy grass. If you saw it you immediately lost the strength in your limbs and felt a great hunger upon you.

Village Wedding

I climbed through mist into a gulley in the crag's
Cleft and, once through, the hags
Ran silver in the suck of peat and sudden
Sheep bucked and ran the beck.

A world of sodden white, cold by the Bride
Stones ledge I turned and took the line
Of wall that falls towards the sour moor and
The smoke-black gritstone chapel on its edge.

Sliding fishlike out of the cloud, I scrambled
Over peat and heather and rambled to the lane
And saw them frozen in the lych gate, a crowd
Of smiles held in a sudden spillage of sun.

Veiled like a nun, she lifted for the lens,
Stood by the fire-faced dazzled boy
Molehanded and all ears who sensed the day
Was given to something older and beyond.

Nosepicking bridesmaids were nudged into place
By an aunt all hat and handbag and new shoes,
And another lick of sun washed them
As the shutter clicked for sideboard frames

And albums and the stares of years to come:
"Oh look at Gran and at her dress. At least you had the sun.
And they'll see the earth-faced farmers in their suits,
The anxious uncles thinking of the pub.

And looking at the flowers and dresses see
Perhaps behind the church the Bride Stones flame
That have seen three thousand years and more
Of such beginnings, such sun-blessed wedding days.

Translating the Bowman

In shadows coaxed out of a quoin
A standing man, bow in hand,
Bas-relief on the wall,
'An Anglo-Saxon archer' said the guide.
The font de-coded showed Cain and Abel,
An angel with a fist of fire, but this
No arrow quiver signifying slaughter,
Just the bow to his mouth:
Gimbaud, lamella, Jew's Harp,
Nothing more murderous than a mouth full of music.

West Col

Prayer flags flap, wands, wind-whipped,
Thread a way by serac and crevasse;
And we, a charm bracelet in Gortex
Wade widdershins through powder snow.

The snow that is a bird whose breast we walk upon.
The snow that is the breath of the sky we stumble through.
The snow that is a white fire lake we burn upon.
The snow that steals our breath and meets the sky's blue bruise.

The snow that suddenly shivers and shifts,
As a murderous grin splits its clown-white face
And, with ribald thunder as the snow-field slides,
The mountain chuckles at its own bad joke.